To the STARS!

The First American Woman to Walk in Space

Carmella Van Vleet
Dr. Kathy Sullivan

Illustrated by **Nicole Wong**

Charlesbridge

Kathy Sullivan loved to explore.

When her dad brought home blueprints of the airplanes he was designing at work, Kathy unrolled the pages and spread them out. She carefully crawled over them, studying the lines and curves.

When she was older, Kathy studied other papers.

Whenever an airplane flew overhead, young
Kathy would stop, look up, and say, "I wonder
where it's going."

She daydreamed about having a pocketful of
airplane tickets. When people asked her what she
wanted to do when she grew up, she'd announce,
"I want to see the whole world!"

But what job lets you do that? Later on, Kathy found out. It started with a ticket and a suitcase.

Houston, TX

Young Kathy loved maps and books and foreign languages, too. Their strange symbols, exotic tales, and musical sounds made her feel like the world was waiting for her. Maybe she'd be a spy or a diplomat. Kathy thought "adventurer" had a nice ring to it.

"Girls don't like those jobs," her friends said.

Most grown-ups told her, "Girls are supposed to be teachers or nurses or moms."

By the time she was an adult, Kathy realized something. "I know what I love, and I'm just going to follow that compass."

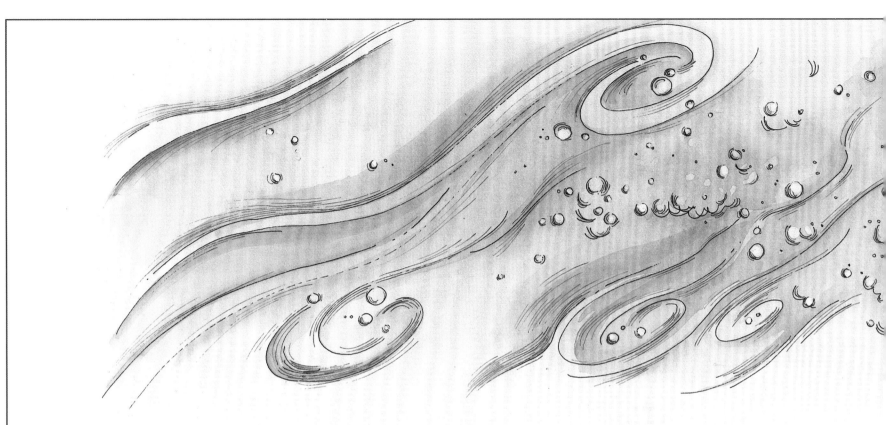

While growing up, Kathy often went fishing with her dad and brother. The three of them climbed in the car and drove through the inky blackness so they could have their lines in the lake when the sun—and the fish—woke up.

Later in the day, when it got so hot that she couldn't stand it a second longer . . .

. . . CANNONBALL!

Kathy delighted in how her arms and legs moved in slow motion underwater.

Kathy loved the water—
even when she was grown.

When Kathy was a teenager, she learned to pilot a plane. The first time she sat in the cockpit, her stomach tied itself in knots. There were so many dials and buttons and numbers!

Years later Kathy studied another instrument panel.

On weekends, when Kathy wasn't at school, she and her dad explored nearby airports. One day they came across a strange red aircraft called a Breezy. As the two of them got closer, they heard the pilot trying to talk his friend into a ride.

"Oh, no," the man said. "I couldn't do that."

Kathy didn't hesitate. "Boy, I sure could!"

"Hop on!" the pilot told her.

Kathy counted down the minutes until they took off.

On another bright blue day, Kathy listened to mission control count down the minutes. "T minus three minutes and counting."

Leaving her dad behind at the airport, Kathy climbed into the seat perched near the Breezy's nose. As the pilot zoomed down the runway, the ground slid away. The wind rushed past her face so fast it pushed her cheeks back. It was like the first day of summer or her birthday or even both at once.

HIGHER!
FASTER!

Sitting on the Breezy was like being on a magical kitchen chair that could fly. Young Kathy looked at the ground below her feet. She felt like she could see the whole world.

And one day, she really did . . .

. . . when she became the first American woman to walk in space.

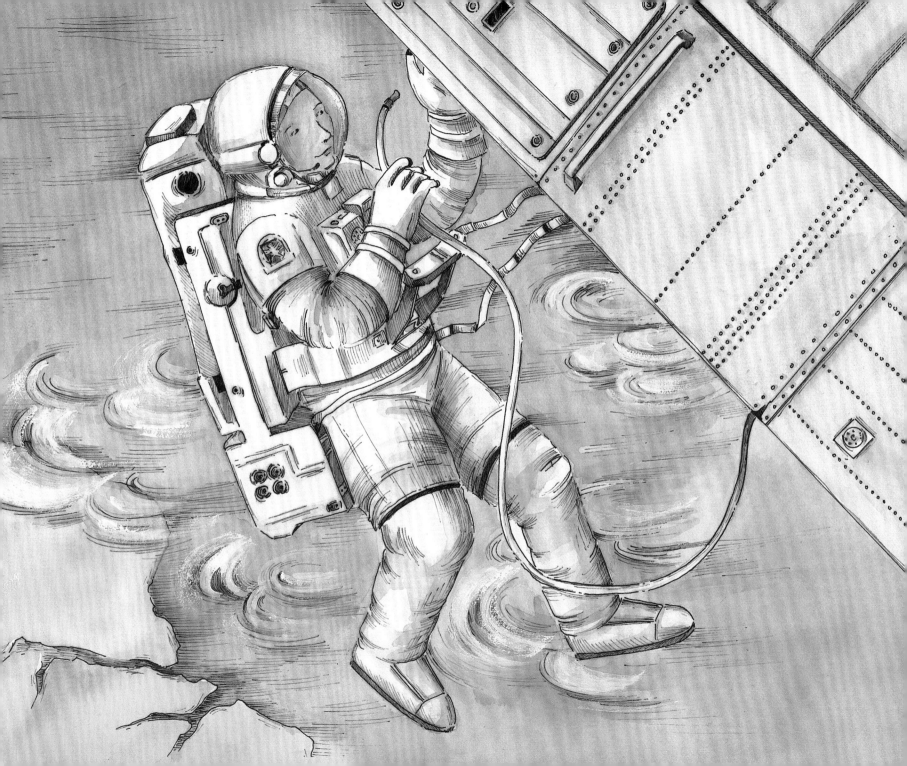

A Note from KATHY

"What do you want to be when you grow up?"

I didn't like this question when I was a little girl. I felt like I was supposed to know exactly what job I wanted, but I didn't. In those days the only acceptable answers for girls were mother, teacher, nurse, or secretary. The things I liked didn't seem to fit into any of those jobs. I liked to explore the woods behind our house and read about faraway places and the lives of adventurous people (mostly men, because only men were supposed to have exciting jobs). I could clearly imagine being someone who knew a lot about the world—geography, geology, history, culture, and languages. I really wanted to be that kind of person, but I had no idea how to make it into a job.

This book tells my story—the story of a dream come true. It tells how I built a path to some of the coolest, most rewarding jobs on (or off!) the planet by following my passion to explore. I worked hard to develop my skills, and I had the courage to set big goals for myself—goals that most people thought a girl could not, or should not, tackle. I hope my story helps you to figure out how to reach for your stars!

More About
KATHY

Dr. Kathryn Dwyer Sullivan was born on October 3, 1951, in New Jersey and grew up in Woodland Hills, California. She had many passions that were considered "boy things" at the time. Thankfully Kathy's parents always supported her interests. Nothing was out of bounds just because she was a girl.

After high school she went to college thinking that maybe she'd become a translator. She was told she had to take some science courses, and soon she was studying oceanography and marine biology. Those classes changed everything. Kathy loved the ocean. She realized that exploring the world could mean much more than living in other cities or countries. It could mean exploring the earth and using science to understand how our planet works. Kathy earned her degree in earth sciences from the University of California, Santa Cruz, and her doctorate degree in geology from Dalhousie University in Nova Scotia, Canada. When her older brother heard that NASA was looking for women scientists, he encouraged Kathy to apply to the program. She knew it was a long shot and had almost forgotten about her application when NASA contacted her. Kathy was actually offered two opportunities after receiving her doctorate. The first was an interview with NASA. The second was to work with deep-sea submersibles. When she called home with the news, her mom asked what it all meant.

"It means I'll either be going ten thousand feet down or two hundred miles up!" Kathy told her.

In the end, the chance to see Earth from space was too much to pass up. Inspired by the missions aboard the *Mercury*, *Gemini*, and *Apollo* that she saw on television as a young girl, Kathy decided she had to try to become an astronaut. More than eight thousand people applied for the first space-shuttle class, but only thirty-five were chosen. Of those, just six were women. Kathy was one of them.

Kathy's first mission, called STS-41G, was aboard the *Challenger*. It was historic for two reasons. It was the first time a space-shuttle crew included two women. (In addition to Kathy, Sally Ride flew on the mission.) It was also historic because Kathy became the first American woman to participate in an extravehicular activity (EVA) during the mission on October 11, 1984. An EVA is commonly referred to as a space walk.

Kathy flew two more missions. This included trips aboard *Discovery* (STS-31), which released the Hubble Space Telescope, and aboard *Atlantis* (STS-45), which helped us better understand the climate and our atmosphere. On *Atlantis* Kathy was the first female payload commander. All in all, she flew three missions and logged more than five hundred hours in space.

In 2004 Dr. Kathy Sullivan was inducted into the United States Astronaut Hall of Fame. She fulfilled her childhood dream and traveled all over the world to visit exotic and mysterious places, including the South Pole.

American Women Firsts in NASA History

The first space shuttle, *Columbia*, launched on April 12, 1981, and had a crew of two. (Later missions had crews of up to eight people.) The final space mission, aboard *Atlantis*, touched down on July 21, 2011. During the thirty-year span of flight, American women accomplished many firsts.

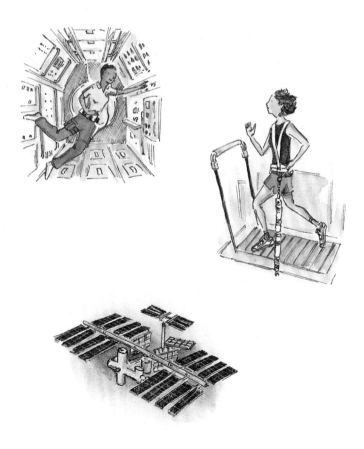

The Women of the First Space-Shuttle Class
(listed in order of their first flight)

Sally K. Ride loved sports when she was a little girl. She also loved science. After she earned her doctorate in physics, she applied to NASA. Reports say she was partially encouraged by Nichelle Nichols, a famous actress from *Star Trek* who recruited women and minorities for NASA at the time. On June 18, 1983, aboard *Challenger*, Dr. Ride became the first American woman to go into space. Dr. Ride was also the first woman to travel to space twice. She flew two missions.

Judith A. Resnik loved math and playing piano as a girl. After earning her doctorate in electrical engineering, she applied to be an astronaut—reports say she was encouraged by actress Nichelle Nichols, too. On August 30, 1984, aboard *Discovery*, Dr. Resnik became the first Jewish woman to go into space. She died along with the rest of the crew in the *Challenger* disaster on January 28, 1986.

Kathryn D. Sullivan became the first American woman to walk in space on October 11, 1984, aboard *Challenger*. She flew three missions.

Anna L. Fisher studied chemistry and medicine. On November 8, 1984, Dr. Fisher was a mission specialist aboard *Discovery*, making her the first mother to go into space. (Dr. Fisher kept a picture of her sixteen-month-old daughter on her shuttle locker during the mission.) Dr. Fisher married a fellow astronaut, Bill Fisher. She flew one mission and is one of the oldest active American astronauts.

M. Rhea Seddon was always interested in space travel but didn't think she would be allowed because she wasn't a man or a pilot. After becoming a physician, she heard NASA was looking for women scientists and applied. During the week of April 12-15, 1985, aboard *Discovery*, Dr. Sheldon used her medical training to conduct the first echocardiogram (a heart test) in space. She and her husband, astronaut Robert Gibson, were also the first NASA classmates to marry. She flew three missions.

Shannon W. Lucid was one of the six women in the first space-shuttle class and, like her female classmates, she was a scientist. Her doctorate was in biochemistry. On December 2, 1996, Dr. Lucid became the first woman to be awarded the Congressional Space Medal of Honor, the highest NASA honor. She flew in five space-shuttle missions, including one that docked with the Russian *Mir* Space Station.

Other Firsts by Women in Space

Kalpana Chawla was born in India and became a US citizen as an adult. Her first name means "imagination," and she dreamed of becoming an astronaut. After earning a doctorate in aerospace engineering, she worked for NASA. On November 19, 1997, aboard *Columbia*, she became the first Indian American woman to go into space. Dr. Chawla flew a second mission aboard *Columbia*. Sadly, on February 1, 2003, the shuttle broke apart before it could land. The accident had no survivors.

Eileen M. Collins wanted to be a pilot from the time she was a young girl and, like Kathy Sullivan, loved to watch planes fly overhead. She earned degrees in science and mathematics. After college she became one of the first women to apply to the United States Air Force Undergraduate Pilot Training program. She was selected by NASA in 1990. On her first spaceflight, launched February 3, 1995, aboard *Discovery*, Collins became the first woman to pilot a space shuttle. And on July 23, 1999, aboard *Columbia*, Collins became the first female shuttle commander. She flew four missions.

Mae C. Jemison wanted to become either a scientist or a dancer when she was little. On September 12, 1992, aboard *Endeavor*, Dr. Jemison became the first African American woman to go into space. (She took a poster of dancers from the famous Alvin Ailey Dance Company with her.) Dr. Jemison is the only astronaut to appear in a *Star Trek* series and was also reportedly one of Nichelle Nichols's recruits. The mission aboard *Endeavor* was her only trip into space.

S. Christa McAuliffe was a New Hampshire social studies teacher who dreamed about space travel. She applied to the NASA Teacher in Space Project, and in 1985, she was chosen from more than ten thousand applicants. She trained with astronauts for 114 hours to prepare for her historic trip. She became the first civilian to travel into space on January 28, 1986, aboard *Challenger*. Tragically, the shuttle exploded shortly after its launch. The accident had no survivors.

Dorothy M. Metcalf-Lindenburger fell in love with the solar system at a young age. She even entered a writing contest in hopes of winning a trip to Space Camp. When she didn't win, her parents sent her anyway. After college she became an earth-science teacher. One day while trying to find an answer for a student, she found an application to become an Educator Astronaut for NASA. On April 5, 2010, aboard *Discovery*, she became the first Space Camp alumna to become an astronaut. It was her only mission.

Ellen L. Ochoa's favorite subject in school was science. She earned her doctorate in electrical engineering and helped invent three optical-engineering systems. Inspired by watching Sally Ride's trip into space, Dr. Ochoa applied to NASA. On April 4, 1993, Dr. Ochoa flew her first mission, serving as a mission specialist aboard *Discovery*. She was the first Hispanic woman to travel into space. Dr. Ochoa traveled into space four times.

Peggy A. Whitson watched the *Apollo 11* moon landing when she was young and thought it was very cool. But she didn't decide to become an astronaut until she graduated from high school and learned about the first female astronauts. She earned her doctorate in biochemistry and soon afterward began working for NASA. On October 12, 2007, she became the first female commander of the International Space Station (ISS). She is also the first woman to be chief of the Astronaut Office, which oversees all astronauts. Dr. Whitson flew two missions.

Sunita L. Williams wanted to be a veterinarian, but she decided to join the Navy instead. There she became a test pilot and later joined NASA. She currently holds the record for most EVAs (space walks) by a woman: seven. She was also the first person to complete a triathlon in space. How? On September 16, 2012, while aboard the International Space Station, she used a stationary bike, a treadmill, and a strength-training machine to mimic swimming. She flew two missions.

For my mom and dad, who always made sure I had books to explore—C. V. V.

To my mother, who gave me permission to fly, and my father, who taught me how—K. S.

In memory of Yvette—N. W.

Text copyright © 2016 by Carmella Van Vleet and Kathryn Sullivan
Illustrations copyright © 2016 by Nicole Wong

Published by Charlesbridge
85 Main Street
Watertown, MA 02472
(617) 926-0329
www.charlesbridge.com

Library of Congress Cataloging-in-Publication Data
Van Vleet, Carmella, author.
   To the stars! First American woman to walk in space/
   Carmella Van Vleet, Dr. Kathy Sullivan; illustrated by Nicole Wong.
      pages cm
   ISBN 978-1-58089-644-3 (reinforced for library use)
   ISBN 978-1-60734-852-8 (ebook)
   ISBN 978-1-60734-853-5 (ebook pdf)
1. Sullivan, Kathryn D.—Juvenile literature. 2. Women astronauts—United States—
Biography—Juvenile literature. 3. Women scientists—United States—Biography—
Juvenile literature. 4. Astronauts—United States—Biography—Juvenile literature.
5. Scientists—United States—Biography—Juvenile literature. I. Sullivan, Kathryn D.,
author. II. Wong, Nicole (Nicole E.), illustrator. III. Title.

TL789.85.S85V36 2016
629.450092—dc23
[B]   2014049183

Printed in China
(hc) 10 9 8 7 6 5 4 3 2 1

Illustrations done in watercolor and ink on Fabriano
   Artistico watercolor paper
Display type set in Elroy by Christian Schwartz Design
Text type set in Triplex by Emigre Graphics
Color separations by Colourscan Print Co
   Pte Ltd, Singapore
Printed by C & C Offset Printing Co. Ltd.
   in Shenzhen, Guangdong, China
Production supervision by
   Brian G. Walker
Designed by Diane M. Earley